RRAIN,
MARS

POEMS

CAROL LYNNE KNIGHT

Carol Lynne Knight (signature)

APALACHEE PRESS

TALLAHASSEE, FLORIDA 2020

Cover image: New impact crater near the Martian equator, 2019
            Courtesy of NASA/JPL-Caltech/University of Arizona
Author photograph: Al Hall
Cover and text design: Carol Lynne Knight
Type Styles: titles set in YanaR and text set Mrs. Eaves;
            dragon fly ornament by Carol Lynne Knight

Library of Congress Cataloging-in-Publication Data
A Fretted Terrain, Like Mars by Carol Lynne Knight – First Edition
ISBN – 978-0-940821-14-9
Library of Congress Control Number: 2019956840

For more information about the author: www.carollynneknight.com

Apalachee Press Inc. is a nonprofit corporation.

For personal orders and information:
apalachee.press2020@gmail.com

Web site: www.apalacheereview.org

Published in the United States
by Apalachee Press
Tallahassee, Florida
First Edition, 2020

For Diane Wakoski

CONTENTS

THE TANGO DANCERS

HOTELS

APARTMENT

REUNION

BODY LANGUAGE

ACKNOWLEDGMENTS

Thanks to the publishers where these poems first appeared, sometimes in slightly different versions.

Another Chicago Magazine: "Meet Me at the Cactus Motel"

Apalachee Review: "Girlfriends Go to the Beach"

Esthetic Apostle: "The Kite Elegies"

Rivet: "Yes, #MeToo"

Scarlet Leaf Review: "Rattle" (as "Meet Me in Las Vegas"), "Meet Me in Cordele," & "Convention" (as "Meet Me in Atlanta")

Black Fox Literary Magazine: "Canvas" (as "Meet Me in Paris")

My thanks to the many friends who listened to these poems, read them, and scribbled helpful and appreciative comments. I am so privileged to live in a supportive and rich literary environment, to be able to share my work with writers like Rick Campbell, Kathleen Laufenberg, Trish MacEnulty, Shannon McEwen, Anne Meisenzahl, Kristine Snodgrass, Jay Snodgrass, Jane Terrell, and Patti White.

Thank you to Barbara Hamby and Jimmy Kimbrell, who agreed within minutes to write back-cover comments. I am so grateful for their thoughtful read and enthusiasm.

Special thanks to the Javas or Java Girls, or various other iterations of the group name, depending on which Tallahassee coffee shop we meet in to share work. We are not sure how to mark the beginning, but it is at least 20 years ago. Thank you Donna Decker, Melanie Rawls, Mary Jane Ryals, and in earlier days, Laura Newton! We read with careful attention. We support. We perform together. We share worries, laughter, and even paint samples. We trade jewelry and clothes and celebrate birthdays. In performance, we dig deeper into each others' poems. We stand on a stage together and honor the words — spoken, spoken word, or sung (not me, so off key).

Also, thank you to Diane Wakoski, whose work inspired me to push further and explore more and whose friendship has enriched my life immeasurably.

The Hambidge Center for the Arts and the Bowers House provided countless hours to write and edit many of these poems. Thank you to the staff and boards of these special places.

My thanks to Apalachee Press and Michael Trammell for bringing this book into the world. My gratitude to my editor, Mary Jane Ryals. This book would not exist without her enthusiasm and encouragement, and her generous gifts of wisdom, time, and expertise.

A FRETTED TERRAIN,
LIKE MARS

RENDEZVOUS

IN THE BACKSEAT

in the backseat, folded
like a lawn chair. jeans so
tight, so hard to wriggle off.

all the barriers to abrupt
passion precisely placed.
this will be no easy ride.

& who's driving &
peering into that oddly
tilted rearview mirror?

all the clouds are flying,
the trees are upside down
& your headliner is torn

in the shape of the panama
canal. & speaking of bodies
of water, your roof is leaking.

romance is drowning in
too many small anomalies
swimming like anemones

into your kisses, & you
didn't shave for me, so
I will have to walk in circles

before I go home to let the bright
red skin on my neck fade before
my father's watchful eyes.

& now a song I want to hear
is wailing on the radio, but your
tongue is in my ear, sounding

like the tide is going out,
& if I could swim through
this traffic, I would backstroke

through the panama canal
& discover the pacific ocean
hidden in your backseat.

or the atomic bomb I was
wishing for in your kiss —
let the fallout begin.

MOON BEAMS

meet me at the old house
across the road. it could be
our secret place, our little motel.

the deranged woman who lived there
died long ago — that house in the woods
with kudzu clawing the walls.

meet me at twilight — the moon
was rosy & round last night. but,
bring a flashlight, just in case

the kudzu goes rogue. you go
first, this could be so romantic?
the moon is shining right through

that skull-shaped hole in the roof.
I've never seen a moon beam before,
but there is a shaking, a shimmering

like a halo falling falling from the sky
& flecking your hair with gold,
even the dust motes are lit up

like the angel hair on christmas trees.
but these motes have sparkling eyes,
as if this place is haunted?

I've never been kissed in a spirit house,
·the moon darting in all directions,
the fireflies singing.

MEET ME AT THE CACTUS MOTEL

— that fake desert tumble-down
tumbleweed destination
when there is nowhere else
to share our bodies. down the road,

not too far, threadbare linens.
we can wreck the room
& never clean up, just leave,
& leave, & leave again.

meet me in the desert of desire.
the window AC rattles like snakes
jittering, a throb of insects drifting
through the broken bathroom vent.

tucked sheets beckon, ravel,
then fall away to reveal a flash flood
of sweat & steam rising from our bodies —
the work of love has spent us.

we sleep a few hours
before slipping
into the parking lot
to leave in separate cars,

to drive home alone,
still riven,
still humming.

CONVENTION
– ATLANTA, 1985

I'll be waiting in the bar
on the 22nd floor —
the one that slowly revolves
atop our convention hotel.
find me on the white
couch facing west.

when we are deep into our boozy preamble,
the one that precedes our brief liaison,
that sculpts a rodin kiss from our implied desires,
I look up & find we are in a different place —
the moonscaped backdrop of your artful
opening line has transformed into skyscrapers.

meet me in atlanta while the full moon
slowly turns away & the skyline, lit
with a mondrian of office windows,
off or on, hovers over the street below,
a bruegel painting strolling on the sidewalk.

soon, a new city emerges below us,
a wild rousseau forest quilts the park
with neon leaves — all forgotten when
we step into the glass elevator & plummet
to the 8th floor — I am dizzy from whiskey
& the vertigo of falling too fast.

meet me in atlanta.
there is chocolate on the pillow,
taut hotel sheets difficult to loosen,
& our clothes falling to the floor

as if we know each other —
meet me before the moon fades

& I remember only the slow tableau
of landscape unfurling, the vanishing walls
of the elevator as we fell — & not
your shoulder, its anonymous
outline against the thin white wall,
or in the morning, the susurrus of
your shower while I grope for my robe
in the room's mauvish twilight.

later, from my balcony, I glimpse
your hawaiian shirt drifting
thru the staid palette
of navy suits at ground level,
& sense that you will also forget
this fleeting brush with moonlight.

FEATHER BOAS
– NEW ORLEANS

on saturday night, we costume ourselves
in pink feather boas, cascades of cheap beads,
& strut down the middle of bourbon street —

remember losing our virginity & lose it again
peeking into the open maw of a strip club,
those slippery bodies teasing the smoke filled air.

dancing with strangers while the chanteuse
on the corner sings like edith piaf, we toss
all our dollars into her tattered guitar case.

after the parade, in our hotel corridor, we stumble
over empty shoes awaiting polish, abandoned trays,
stacked with gilded plates, glasses & forks akimbo,

leftover wine staining rumpled white napkins. we loiter
on the terrace, then find our bed. still wrapped
in feather boas, our bodies twine together —

dreams swirling like confetti till sunday morning.
we breakfast early along the river, dust our fingers
with powdered sugar from beignets dipped in coffee

slightly bitter, wander across jackson square,
its lawns littered with the refuse of last night's revelers.
there is a riff of trombone ghosting in the alley,

our pink feathers purling from the balcony,
echoes of song adrift on the sidewalk.

GIRLFRIENDS GO TO THE BEACH

ONE
when we go to the beach
the ride is the most fun,

sudden freedom away from
the house — where my skin is always

too small. now, the need to answer
& comply is ground into the asphalt.

here we go! hand out the window,
air pushing against it as we speed.

the snarl of wind rolling over my skin.
I let it lift my arm as if I can fly away.

look, I have grown feathers.

TWO
radio music surrounding us —
a sonic swirl, the air vibrating

with heartbeat, the car rocking
at the stop light as we dance,

bouncing like beach balls
out of the car, then back in

just before the light turns green —
all of us landing upside down

in the back seat, laughing
& wriggling to be right side up,

like bath toys bobbing to the surface.
we defy gravity & traffic & keep dancing.

THREE
we are hot tamales on the ride home —
red skin, pink skin, unburned handprint

from sunscreen carelessly placed,
still basking in freedom & sand,

salty skin, stringy hair. lolling
not dancing, crooning not rocking.

someone's head on my shoulder,
soft breath, a little curl of seaweed

tangled in her hair, wet towels on the seat,
warm sodas passing around, windows

down, an irish lullaby sung slow enough
to be off key, green lights all the way.

we're dragging back in that sweet,
sassy way of almost sundown,

wafer of moon chasing us home.

CANVAS
– PARIS

meet me in paris, this old city
that I have only dreamed in books,
or films with clacking sprockets — images,
breathless & subtitled in a language
of confused desire & ennui.

meet me in paris,
where my dreams will take us
to blanche station,
up winding stairs to our flat
on a cluttered alley —
lines of laundry flaunting wind,
lullaby from an open window,
a charcoal sketch of
our chair in the corner,
our tossed clothes
in chiaroscuro.

take me to the boulevard montmartre,
below the window where pissaro
stood for hours as rain fell
& umbrellas began to chatter
across his canvas. find a café
away from the traffic
of horse-drawn carriages
& teeming crowds of parisians —
where my accent is perfect,
& cats doze under the tables.

STOLEN
– VANCOUVER

I stand where the mirror lets my clothes
fall to the floor — in my two hands,
flower or dagger. but soon the chinese
restaurant, steaming rice & dumplings.

steal a spoon

for me, for breakfast tomorrow in my room,
for all the soup to come, so I will remember
the crowded sidewalks & distant green,
the harbor apparent in a whiff of brine.

buy me a fish

for dinner, served on white plates
with gilded rims, three forks
placed on the left like fractured combs.
the server will light a candle when we arrive.

hail a taxi

to stanley park, that green peninsula
on the map. let your hands create
a memory in the back seat — the driver
a witness to love dissembling.

take a photo

beneath the cedars hiding the sky,
soughing with breezes from english bay.
our walk in the rainforest almost enchanted,
our kiss like a conjured good bye.

leave me

at the train station in the morning
with a hurried embrace,
a low whistle, a chuff of steam —
a face that would weep if time allowed.

RATTLE
– LAS VEGAS

taxi from the airport, past
neon façades, past
country club green,
past infrequent palms posed
at motels with murky pools
& sagging lounge chairs,
the painted sand & sage.

keep driving

till the desert
almost swallows the road.
turn left when there
is nowhere else to turn.
drive to the end of the cul de sac
with the bent palm tree,
its brown fronds weeping
into a sepia yard of gravel.

enter the blue house with the open door.
mirrors that line the hall will distort
your reflection as you walk
toward a sunken living room.

don't go there.

face left & climb
the spiral staircase to the loft.
in this false twilight —
for I have shut the sun
with ragged blankets hung
over the windows —

I will be waiting supine,
my bed balanced
on concrete blocks.
the ac will rattle like
early morning sanitation trucks.

ignore the clamor.

open the jeweled box
on the nightstand.
inside, the secret that frees
our skin to its slick & sweat,
lays bare a fragile mercy, once
hidden in our hollows & curves,
conjures a baobab tree —
how its leaves shade our bed,
our oasis in this desert.

FRACTURE
– SAVANNAH

moss twists its gray floss to twitch
in the lazy breeze. marble angels
preside over the river as we meander
in a molasses haze — its slant light.

the cat sleeping on johnny mercer's grave
greets you like a familiar, slinks between
your ankles. we sit to share the shade —
tall grasses rasp & purl at the edge of the river.
I tuck my hand over your arm & imagine I am

quaintly gloved, cinched into a flounced
& swaying gown for our promenade
in whitefield square. its gazebo is haunted
with azaleas & the fettered ghosts of slaves.
we stroll into the past, the centuries of magnolias

& courtly soirées, the past fractured by movies
& preserved in weathered stones etched
with fading forevers & awkward cherubs.
to loosen this corset of longing, this strangle

of gloves & curtsies, we retreat to our beige motel
near the interstate. I kiss you in a dialect of drawl,
touch you as if we have already passed on — my hand
like smoke, your mouth a phantom. no buried respite

or even casual grief — only the whining dirge
of a truck shifting gears on the overpass,
& our regrets carefully folded & packed for home,
that long morning drive, that familiar silence.

AT THE DUTCH MOTEL,
– TAMPA

with its tiny windmill,
with its rough bathroom door,
stuck closed & shutting me
out of our guest room,
until you pull it open,

laughing. the bed,
a tossed affair
where we sleep,
your so-young body
next to mine

that is so yearning
for skin & abandon
that I have driven
250 miles to
find you again.

these days
I am untamed —
meaning lost,
in human terms,
forsaken
& seeking.

you wake,
your body
so lovely in
the half light.

SHADE
– MIAMI

stretched out under the sea grapes
banked above the beach, I wait
in the shade for your wet body to return,
glistening with salt from the atlantic.

while the sun dances adagio, we wade
along the strand, a wash of broken
shells & seaweed swirling at our feet,
a liquid, rhythmic slap of waves.

we doze & dream beneath the sea grapes,
their leaves red-singed & ruffling.
a sudden wind foreshadows rain
& we wait for the thunder to shake us,

for lightning, for a brief interlude.
only you & I on this deserted beach —
our singular kiss unleashes its own
bright spark, our singe & fire.

CARRARA
– ROME

I am a fold of marble on the bridge
of angels, waiting to be shaped
in your bernini hands. come to me
on the worn & weary travertine
spanning the tiber — its yellow face.

ignore the fake gladiators outside
the coliseum & stroll the arcade with me —
glimpse the memories of vestal virgins,
their ghosts gliding beneath the arena.
count the steps & revere the stones that remain.

at st. peter's door, whisper to me of the pieta.
let her scarred carrara flesh be healed
& curse the hammer that severed her perfect
fingers — now mended, they still hold the exquisite
joy of michelangelo's homage to light & flesh.

find a small pensione on a quiet piazza,
so we can sleep till noon undisturbed, our sheets
heavy, like the brocade skirts of carravagio's
penitent magdalene. wake me

with hot cappuccino. embrace me
in the forbidden waters of trevi fountain
before we escape the polizia, but leave
behind our coins — a wish for more,
a payment for joy.

THE ROAD TO TUSCALOOSA

the late afternoon
solstice, fog blending trees
in distant shades
of inky viridian, past the swale,
to faraway gray, fading fast.

driving toward you
in heavy mist or
is that uncommitted rain?
everything wet
and suspended in half-
light, impatient
for sunset to paint

the blackish silhouette
of pines & cedar
at the edge
of the world, to
press a knife
into the thick impasto
of evening, briefly
obscured in the glare

of a passing car.
mist revealed
in street lights,
their yellowish breath
leavening the golden
time before this
briefened twilight
on the road,
this dream time.

LOST LUGGAGE
– AUSTIN

in the tundra of my hotel room,
though clothed, I feel half dressed, adrift
without my luggage that flew to atlanta.
I will be waiting without my special soap,

without my toothbrush or sexy shoes.
through my smudged window on the seventh floor,
we can watch the mexican bats rise up from
the congress avenue bridge — a shimmering cloud

of hunger etching the sky. lady bird lake reveals
herself in the zig-zags & jitters of sunset
in lamplight scrawled across the water.
we can walk to the other hotel for champagne,

& barbecue & tacos — little bites of spice!
strolling back, grackles blather & squawk
in the trees outside the convention hall —

louder than the drunken poets on the corner.
wake me in austin, where I am grateful
for the suitcase that arrives in the morning,
for toothpaste & mascara, for a chinese robe

I can remove when I choose — perhaps tonight,
after the bats return to their roost, after more
champagne, & maybe those slow smoked ribs.
after we have joined the chorus of raucous grackles

as we walk back, maybe then I will slip
into my robe, & then slip out.

CHEVY IMPALA
– NASHVILLE

meet me in nashville
where the bar is open late,
the music makes you sigh,
& drinks are two for one.

I'll be leaning on the polished hood
of a '59 chevy impala convertible
parked inside the bar — the hub
of the prowl — & waiting
for a slow song so I can drape
myself on your muscled shoulder
& explore our mutual curves.
after the dance, we can make out
in the impala's back seat,
& I'll remember fred & mike,
but never ask the names you might recall
as the disco ball shatters above us.

later, we will run across the parking lot
as rain begins to sputter on cars,
to gutter & pool,
& our bucket-seat-gear-shift-
semi-clothed attempts at intimacy
end in tangles of denim & laughter,

& then in conversation that lasts
until the lot empties at 4 a.m. —
the deserted gravel,
the smoke-fed glow
of streetlights tracing
a fretted terrain,
like mars.

MOMENTUM
– NEW YORK CITY

meet me in manhattan, where the crosswalks
seethe with momentum, where we shoulder
our murmured affections, enjoy the jostle
& forced embrace of the crowd.

in the subway to jackson square, I grab
the same pole, shake with the rails' hum
& clatter, sway to the lonesome blues the man
in a tattered sweater hums from his corner seat.

at the indian restaurant, we banter with friends
we never see, but love in that cross-country way,
laughing till midnight. rick plays the harp like a train
at rush hour while the waiter nods in time
& tips more wine into our glasses.

a walk in a downpour — a glacial hotel.
let your kiss linger after I fuss with the key card.
let a sweet silence follow the hollow hammer
of the door latching when we part,

let it fold into my suitcase,
ready for tomorrow's shuttle.
& steam in the coffee waiting
at the airport in charlotte,

& when I unpack tomorrow night,
let its golden hush touch me
with your scent,
my heart like glass.

TROIKA
– CHICAGO

at the convention center in chicago,
they entomb the book fair in the basement
& the literati stroll & smoke outside,
while the open mouth of a winter cobra
hisses down every caverned street,

& the taxis swallow poets,
who would never find the restaurant —
would miss the italian pies & slabs
of corned beef, the german beer,
& irish whiskey neat.
we tell the driver,
"russian tea time,"

& dine on borscht & crusty bread,
cabbage stuffed with savory beef.
my grandmother's accent rises
from the grand black coats that sweep
the floor in the hatcheck. we feast
while violins recall zhivago
at the train station & a troika
sliding thru the snow, its shaking bells.
an uproar in the next room — vodka-fueled
toasts that shake the walls. "na zdorovye!"
the glasses clink & tip to health.

walking back along michigan avenue,
the night sky opaque, glittering snow
restless on the asphalt. an ice-sculptured
elephant & octopus waltz in grant park
beneath its baroque lanterns & lamplight,
as our shadows lace back & forth on the sidewalk.

so familiar now, the hotel's long corridors
& balky key cards. the sheets will be freezing,
& the thermostat stuck on arctic —
a pretense for sipping from tiny bottles
of bourbon, for a hot shower together,
for sauna, & for steam, for refuge
from the snow that swallows stars.

WATER LILIES
– NEW YORK CITY

how we met at the MOMA,
serpentine lines weaving
across 53rd street. monet, long
passed, his water lilies flooding the walls,

& I was submerged, floating in a river
of chroma & shimmer, drifting under
the bridge built over the pond at giverny,
swooning at paint applied like dreams.

you reveled, watching me, stood back,
with hands tucked in your pockets,
talking quietly to the guard. I wondered
if you could protect such happiness —

the floating colors like flutes & pipes
at the gates of dawn, the journey down
the river, damp & delirious. vapors over
the blossoms, leaves spreading like umbrellas

over the water, or gondolas for dreamers.
when we left, I was still in a trance,
barely noticing your hand. how could
I ignore such careful regard, the tether

that kept me safely on the ground? my mind
jolted back into my body when thirty frenzied
young girls ran down the street toward
the corner hotel, a camera man chasing behind.

were they were fans of monet, crazed by his paint?
no, you nodded. the guard had told you about

the beatles & how to access their hotel's hidden entrance.
all week, their presence causing another

kind of delirium — so loud & chaotic.
we strolled away from the warwick hotel —
you the guide & me drifting back into monet's
conjures of color & grace.

GILT

– LONDON

face east at dawn on london bridge.
await that turner-&-monet moment,
painted when the thames reflects
a cadmium red, boats dark against
a wash of gray & prussian blue.

turn my face into your collar as anne
boleyn offers a coin to the executioner
& lays her head on the block —
an intrigue of courtiers destined
to end beneath a trembling hand.

kiss me as juliet — so eager & half sketched,
girl with a poisoned fate. as my balcony lists
on the delicate scaffolds of passion,
step into the spotlight & seek me
with shakespeare's vault of words.

reach for my hand beneath whistler's table.
serve me tarts with a golden fork
& follow me to the peacock room —
gilt & feathers overwhelming our embrace
while I boast that my wit exceeds our desire.

tangle me in the swirling ink of aubrey beardsley's
skirts. I could be a salome revealed in erotic tattoos
and blossoms, enslaved by his lines that tether me
to his page. hold up the mirror to his profile, so like
mine — then seek the india ink, its dark caress.

find me during the blitz, my movie
of london in black & white terror.

crush my body against the dank wall
of the subway tube, its dull concussion.
carry me home thru smoldering gray fire,
hissing smoke — light a cigarette & keep
changing the reels, our story still unwinding.

GRANITE
– CRESTED BUTTE

outside the gunnison library,
I first hear the news:
my mother has passed away,
the grieving has begun.

I cannot breathe, & cannot mourn
where snow falls on mountain tops
in late june, or even where lupine tempts
the swallowtails & sulphurs.

in the rockies, granite faces still scarred
with ice surround us. a shadow of clouds
is choreographed by unseen angels
of wind & sun. the silence is glacial,
while phlox begins to bloom.

riding up the stolid face
of the red lady, swaying
in her lift chair like wind dolls,
our legs dangling & free —
we depart where the snow
still lies in shady drifts
& the trail climbs
upward, an altitude of sighs.

cruising down the mountain
on a winding state road, we follow the slate
till it converges with east river, its waters
rampant & wild & threatening to overflow —
to close the bridges of lost canyon.

in gunnison, I can breathe & wander thru the safeway
without gasping. the tacit palisades of granite leave me
yearning for the susurrant sound of ocean,
the rhythm of the atlantic waves that she loved.

but then, the wind in the harebells & the wild roses,
rustling in the spires of lupine.

RAIN,

from seattle driving north —
chinese landscapes
hang from the sky, villages
mist above the clouds.

along the skagit river,
eagles drift & dive over
water writhing with the silver
of salmon, their spawn & lust.

then, flat fields quilted
with fat tulips, acres of red,
then yellow, then white —
white as snow geese resting
on a fallow patch, hundreds in chorale —
their libretto of bray & stutter.

atop the fiords that bank
the pacific — cerulean tints
the shallows below, the spruce
& hemlock clinging to rock.
even thru the impossible clouds
damp in our hair — the azure sea.

ferry me to oblivion
on the olympic peninsula
the waters of puget sound,
a gray chop, whale songs
rumored in the wake.

let me hear their cries of sorrow
& jubilation. let their liquid voices silence
the first uncertainties of cancer awaiting
me when the plane lands tomorrow.

a splendor of green,
the waxen glisten of cedar,
the sadness of clear cut
hillsides, this elastic time

between the fiords —
a delicate center line twisting,
with a guard rail tracing
the edge of a sapphire lake,
the speed in the curves, a sublime terror.

walking rialto beach, a bleached roar of waves
arrives with rhythmic precision.
worn stones squeak under our feet.
a rendezvous, where rain forest gives way
to the meandering mouth of the hoh,
a river beyond the mountain of mythical trees —

later, we can sleep in the terminal
until the redeye boards
for the other end of world.

AT THE EDGE OF THE MEADOW,
— Colorado

as you step from the road,
the air electrified — scant charges
drawing you & the bees into the field —
the sugared air hints of nectar & possibility.

I wear a red dress so you can find me
at the verge of the meadow & sense
my yearning beyond the columbine.
find me in our forest of atomic desire.

make your way thru the fairy slipper
& ground cherry. I am waiting, & the bees
are hungry — dipping into the lupine,
ignoring the phlox & my red skirt.

I am so like a bee that you will comb my hair
& find honey, perhaps my sting. you will know me
by my folding red silk, my nuclear torrent,
my waft of impulse. quicken your steps

thru the bitterroot, the fireweed, the yarrow.
I am waiting in the shade of aspen & pine,
in my bed of fallen needles. I am on my back

& wondering about the scent of you & two men,
who would sometimes meet me in the morning,
fingers wandering beneath my red silk,
bodies shattered under the twisting branches.

my cheating hands graze your cheek, a parting
among the gaura at the edge of the road, my red skirt
clinging, my singe extinguished, a scent of lavender.

MEET ME IN CORDELE

meet me in cordele.
the chinese restaurant is mediocre,
but good for hunger & foreplay, eyes over
lo mein, hands like shadow puppets
playing on the red dragon in the window.
fortune cookies that promise
your conquest & success.

meet me in cordele.
the interstate will whine
in the parking lot,
muffling our first few minutes
of awkward conversation —
happy hour traffic on friday night
in tifton slowed to a stutter,
I-75 a crazed blur of rain

& condensation, like our skin,
last time — slick, bright,
bluish with tv flicker.

there will be nothing there but me,
no distractions, except the hotel television.
perhaps that lioness — her tongue
grooming her mate as
I gaze across the sheets.

meet me in cordele,
meet me when you hunger,
when the lions mate.
meet me halfway.

THE TANGO DANCERS

See *Notes* on page 66 for descriptions of tango steps.

HOTELS

1. STRAND

how we left the party before midnight
to search the beach, its strand of packed sand,

its shark's teeth & sea turtles digging nests
under a lotus moon. how rain began

to pock the beach, warning us away
with heat lightning curling around the bay.

how we sat in the hotel bar till closing
& then in the lobby, afraid to part & let
the conversation end — like film credits
silently rolling. but, we still did not trust

the elevator, floor by floor, its private space,
our choices when the doors slid open.

2. THRESHOLD

how we left the party after midnight
& thought we would walk to the pier,

pelicans sleeping on pilings, gulls
keening above, & a padlocked gate.

nearby — a bench, one lantern shining,
palmettos rattling in the wind.

how the mist sputtered into rain
as we strolled back to the hotel,

the bellhop dozing near the front desk,
our clothes dripping, our feet bare —

we pushed our separate buttons
in the elevator. when the doors slid open

for me, how I hesitated, then stepped
over the threshold — you almost shrugged,

then reached for my hand as the doors
began to close, and now the choice

seemed to be mine —
but that shrug, that shrug.

3. TRYST

how we missed the party that started at 9
on the veranda — both lost while searching

the hotel for the elusive outdoor fête.
both jet lagged & our bodies telling us

it is past midnight & time for a nightcap —
we followed the tarnished gold signs pointing

to a hotel bar. how we arrived from different
elevators. bumped our heads on fake tiffany shades

as we settled into a booth — craft beer,
salty popcorn, & laughter about the hotel's

quirky floor plan, how we traded quips
until we were laughing more than talking.

how night became morning, 4 a.m.
in my time zone, how I wondered

about those elevator doors as we closed
the bar, singing a sad & off-kilter version

of "blue moon," lingering on a sofa in the lobby,
still wondering whether we would leave

the elevator together — he seemed a kindred spirit,
& I began to wish we would somehow progress

to a sleepy denouement, a tryst, & then began
to laugh at these words so hard that

I was wheezing & tearing — a silly drunk, I guess.
he pulled me into the glass elevator looming

outside the bar, a dizzy climb to my floor.
as I tumbled out like a rag doll, he caught me,

half carried me to my room. tryst, tryst,
I half said, as I produced my key card.

the bed seemed to rise up to meet me.
I felt my shoes being removed before

I drifted into sleep. In the morning,
a note on my night stand. *Mon amour,*

meet me for brunch on the veranda.
yes, I have found it!

4. IDIOT

how we almost missed the airport shuttle,
how we put off packing & dressing.

& then the sumo wrestling match with my suitcase,
how I dithered & drifted as the luggage

was stowed & daydreamed about my ticket
changing to match his — a terrible yearning

began to wrap doubt around
my ankles & trip my tongue.

how I imagined him relieved, since
he would be embracing an idiot (me)

at the gate, & happily saying farewell.
all these doubts before realizing

he was planning our next rendezvous,
suggesting we take tango lessons

before we meet in september —
a way to continue seduction

in another time zone, another party,
the same brilliant stars over the veranda.

5. KISMET

how we met in another hotel,
danced our first tango together

on that veranda, my nervous laughter
before that first hot *promenade,*

a sweeping *planeo.* how our feet
slid across the floor as one.

the *media luna* with an elegance I had
dreamed about in the dance studio,

but never achieved. our *giros & boleos*
almost perfection — how this dance

was kismet, a word I had never thought real
until the music began & the floor electrified

our feet, kismet — kismet in every touch.
our heart beats aligned to the *bandoneón* —

his body cleaving to mine, the lovely shock of it,

lustrada, sentada, deep into, then out of our bodies —
an ether of desire, our toes, our shoulders, our hips,

& hands, our gaze entwined in the dance.
how the *volcado,* the fall, his embrace & catch

as the music ceased, left our bodies
sublimely entangled.

6. VERANDA

how the veranda's intensity lingered
as we strolled the darkened golf course,
the softened night, the hotel's manicured grass,
sand traps shining in moonlight that illuminated

our image, how the moon's path on the lake
painted us as one rippling reflection,

fastened by her light.

APARTMENT

1. LAST HOTEL

how my hand grips the coffee mug, seeking
warmth & steam on the morning after our last hotel.

my familiar kitchen, my breakfast, late morning,
the faint rhythm of a tango around my table —

my legs, our *promenades* on the veranda,
desire — absently stirring in cream, recalling

the jolt of the last *volcado* — the falling
& the rescue, like love — his arm catching

me just before I drop to the floor, my trust
that he will, his silence as he lifts me.

the *bandoneon's* last note.

2. ONE APARTMENT

how we left the party early or missed it,
dancing in seattle & denver, tampa

& savannah, miami or LA, closing hotel bars with long
sad songs, elevator doors sliding open,

stubborn room keys, lost luggage. but this?
this is not a tango. how can it end well?

& yet we must try! a courthouse wedding
in the city, one apartment for two. can we

transform a tango-waltz-redeye romance
into an everyday-breakfast-in-the-same-city

marriage? who will shop for food & who
will take out trash? will my cat stop hiding,

hissing at him? will he fuss at me to squeeze
the toothpaste from the bottom? yet we must

keep our tryst & tango on a veranda
while our wild-blue-yonder is tamed.

3. FROTH

how I fume in the kitchen
when he laughs again —

talking to his ex-wife for an hour
about how to fix the ice maker,

and that terrible neighbor with six kids
and a rooster in the back yard.

waiting dinner in the kitchen, I have destroyed
almost a dozen paper napkins as I listen, shredding,

twisting tiny bits of paper without realizing. paper
suffers like worry beads when my hands are idle.

how I counter with a kitchen symphony:
banging cabinet doors, the blender

on high, the chop, chop, chopping —
that salad should be dead by now,

its lettuce like slaw, the tomatoes
practically puréed, the dressing beaten,

& blended till it froths, the pans deliberately
dropped with a thrilling clatter. then a meal shared

in silence, an aria of dishes thrown in the sink,
my knife screeching & scraping across my plate.

4. TECTONIC

makeup sex, intense like nightmares
or the opposite, but which?

sigh, & the ceiling sighs, too —
criss-crossed with a sweep of headlights

& slatted shades — a jagged sketch
for our discontent, a *boleo,* tectonic

plates shifting beneath the sheets,
an earthquake hurling a tsunami,

or collapsing an interstate highway,
still heaving, still crashing.

5. LIKE RAIN

sigh, & the floor seems to rumble & groan —
goodbye sex, skin on fire, every cell reaching.

the slatted shades like eyes staring
from the streetlight, brightening the room —

daggers of light slicing the wall, purging
desire from this doubtful moment.

a wish that this is makeup sex, & not goodbye,
so similar, like a hurricane beneath the sheets,

moments of calm, the deceptive eye,
bands of tears like rain on radar, a tidal

surge carries away the shelter of the bed.
a drowning. & then waking to a new landscape.

6. STORY

it was a story we told together —
while he hovered on the arm of the sofa.

how we left the party early in dozens
of hotels, preferred the back booth

in the lounge for our foreplay — joked about
our counterparts in that alternate universe,

in an alternate hotel where they never stepped
off the elevator together, lived a sad life

with no tangos, no verandas,

no golf course waltzes — so much they would miss,
how we would smugly wish them well

in their fringe existence — so dull compared
to our tangos & cosmopolitan trysts.

it was our story & we told it together,
& now — this morning, a house without footfall.

it is like a *bandoneón* has collapsed
with a prostrated moan, been abandoned

on a familiar chair, the absence of music
apparent in its flattened bellows,

its off-kilter silence. it was our story —
we told it together & now, we do not.

7. FIREFLIES

how the veranda collapsed in our hearts,
a thousand sighs at its loss, no more

promenades, boleos, no media lunas,
how the tango has fled, how the ache

is long & deep, the evidence there ever was
a tango, like fireflies on a distant field, their faint flash

the only blaze remaining, how I sigh & the closet
seems to huff & rattle the empty coat hangers,

how pushing my clothes into that gaping space
is like a failed volcado, "the man causes

the woman to fall off her axis" & today abandons her,
turns away, shuts her red front door — shut.

REUNION

1. LATTE

ten years pass like a peel of lime
ever curling, a little zest, a long, slow
martini. the *media luna*, the *promenade*
forsaken, hotels in distant cities,

ghosted — a fabric of cobwebs upholstering
the lobby, paint peeling from the veranda,
its invisible stars fracturing, like the pattern
swirling in her latte amidst the café chatter

& sassy music of women laughing
in a back booth, but she is lost in *neruda* —
a napkin twining between her fingers
as she reads, feet fidgeting.

he has come to the wrong café, about
to turn & leave — across the room, a woman
in half profile, her hand absently twisting
a shred of paper napkin, bent over

a book. as he crosses the room — flash-
backs of that red shut door. after threading
around four tables, he hesitates, a stillness
& then somehow, he is standing close enough

to see the pink pearl of her nail polish.
still wondering, until she looks up.
she smiles. after all, she has been
reading *neruda*. with the book tucked

away, she is ready to flee if that shut
door shuts again. she rises to meet him,
recalling the tango — the tango,
that elegant beast.

2. VOLCADO

the sassy laughter abates in the back
booth as he offers his hand. he whispers,
volcado. she startles, no! he leans in,
a murmur of touch on her back —
volcado! she places her hand
on his shoulder, remembers
the *bandoleon,* its passion.
he pulls her off axis.

she trusts him as she falls, remembering
the pulse & beat — it fills the café as
she breathes again, freely for the first time
since her red door shut behind him.

there is applause, & just as they did
at the last hotel, they bow. they sit.
the server brings more latte, a pattern
of hearts drifting on the surface.

the steam rises as they drink,
rises like the scent of star jasmine
climbing a trellis on the veranda,
its blossoms in her hair, so long ago.

3. LITTLE SHOCKS

under the table, her ankle turns,
almost sliding into a *promenade,*
the pleasure of recall & the forgotten
discord, strands of memory touching

each familiar nerve. little shocks ride up
her spine as they finally begin to speak —
their words tumbling, so many questions:
how are ... what have you ... how is the cat?

do you still dance? a caress of time,
as if the first time is now & the cafe
is a hotel bar after midnight.
she briefly mourns the wasted years

of perfect order without him. now
she faces him — her one true friend.
some think the tango is about desire
but she knows it is the eyes, how he

recognized all that she was as they
turned as one in a *boleo,* on the face
of the moon, that split second
of knowing — a potion, an addiction.

4. WISTERIA

the cafe's patio, enclosed in wisteria vine,
begins to glow as servers light candles
in crystal lamps. in the center, a small fountain
hushes outside traffic. he leads her thru the maze
of chairs, to a table outside,

holding her hand, almost afraid to let go,
both laughing about a similar place
at that last hotel. before they sit, they
execute a perfect *planeo,* she circling

him as he pivots, till they collapse
into their chairs with a half sigh/half groan.
the long-ago wisteria twining the veranda rail,
the cave of lavender blossoms

enclosing them. in recall — there was a kiss,
like crystal, a slow & ethereal tango, their last —
lights shimmering below the indigo sky
that night — that scent, an intoxicant, a potion

of honey & clove —
the whip & dizzying
spin of their *boleos.*

5. NERUDA

the wait staff begins to quench the candles
and refill the salt & pepper shakers, some sit
at an empty table assembling place settings,
wrapping sets of utensils in linen napkins.

the decision to leave no longer theirs, they stand
& gather what they brought — she, the book,
a shopping bag, & now hesitation. but his old imprint,
a slight shoulder lift & nod, summons her to follow,

a migration of the heart — now on the sidewalk
outside the cafe, he bends to kiss her,
as she juggles her purse & keys & questions
still unanswered — her book tumbles

into the street, lies open to neruda's
"song of despair." *ah,* he says,
you clung to desire! she blushes,
& leans into his kiss, her body

returning to him before she thinks about
the disruption to her quiet, almost boring,
life, every object just so, her cat the only
thing that moves in her apartment.

the tango they danced in every room,
faded into the wallpaper. and now he has
returned, walked thru her red front door,
& into her kitchen. his lank body sprawling

on a wooden chair, he offers to cook —
she nods. he reaches for the skillet,
still stored in the bottom drawer, grabs
the olive oil & pulls a steak from the fridge.

amused, he asks, *did you know I was coming?*
she answers, *oh! yes! of course!* confounded
by why she had actually thawed the steak.
there is a certainty in his movements,

he smiles at the heap of garlic, still
in a blue bowl by the toaster. the cat
nudges his leg & purrs. she has been
waiting for him. he sings an old high-

school song, *blue moon, you saw me
standing alone!* as he chops the pearled
cloves & pounds the steak.
there is music, again.

6. STILL BURNING

a crystal hurricane lamp,
its illumination, so kind
to her aging skin, still burning
on the porch after dinner.

each spoonful of flan tasted more
slowly as she counts the new scars
he has not seen, the trust she has not
offered anyone. fear is a viper

curled in her lap, that soft hiss

growing louder, the half empty closet,
his vacuous ex-wife, the broken dishes.
while he rinses the pans, she pushes
away from the table, slams the two doors

between them till she is seated on the edge
of the tub, furious at him for leaving,
at the cat for jumping into his lap tonight.
she is ready to assault the stranger

who tripped her outside the café last year
& left a four-inch scar on her ankle.
she hears him humming & imagines
his hands finding the scar as they undress

tonight. but that will never happen!
now the viper is more like the fiery dragon
in china delight's front window.

7. PORCELAIN

she drums the porcelain, wondering
how to get out of the bathroom with dignity.
the cat whining at the door & the voice
of *neruda* interrupts her pathetic thoughts,

there was grief & ruins & you were the miracle.
he is still singing & the cat's paw is poking
under the door, beckoning. *ah neruda!*
and the tenderness, light as flour & as water.

she stretches, uncurls her hands
from the cold white tub. *ah, neruda,*
I think I know what you meant. she stands,
arches her back, & lets the cat in.

he calls from the kitchen. she answers.

8. PRISM

the *volcado* at the cafe,
its ease & memory —
like a prism casting desire
& trust across the wall in waves

of indigo & blue, a flutter of red,
the quiet bedroom, the slip
of linen, then silk, the hurricane
lamp, its amber light,

the release of clasps,
the floor, its trail of clothes.
she recalls the falling
and the arch of her back,

for him she kills
the fear, the hiss.

9. WREN

a wren hovers at the window
tangoing with light falling thru the shades —
morning, morning — the night like indigo
and lace tatted with silver thread,

& now, the raveling — something
is hissing under her pillow — only an
indent left on his, empty — the viper waking,
the warm sun insisting at the sill.

& then, a wordless song from the kitchen,
coffee bubbling & groaning into the carafe,
the wren climbing the screen, plucking with her
tiny talons, the cat aroused & pawing the shade,

the scent of oranges & coffee,
the wren, the cat, the song, his song.

10. ORANGE & MINT

at breakfast: the coffee, the wren
that continues to dance at the window,
now more than a shadow, but still
umber & tossing light in delicate

flurries across the porch. how fresh
oranges & mint had been conjured
from her meager stock. how she

savored each slice. each strawberry,
unadorned, but perfect & red.
how he will return in june.

11. ELEVATOR DREAMS

she waits & dreams of elevator
doors, their sliding mirror as they shut.
the smudged image, sometimes with him,
hands palm-to-palm, or separate

as she hesitates, then enters alone,
leaning on the back wall, the elevator's
distorted voice announces the closing,
then chimes at her floor. as the doors

slide open, the room service trays
stacked in the hall, the crumpled napkins,
the narrow & endless corridor, the hollow
click of the hotel door, the chill in the room,

the bleached white sheets. the wren wakes
her every morning, plucking the screen
like a dissonant harp, sun rising
in the southeast — scent of oranges

& coffee, the tick & ring of a spoon inside
a cup, the stirring. the singing.
she rises.
it is june.

12. THE MILONGA

on the dance floor — its polished shine,
two hands clasp, so familiar,
the elegance ascends as he presses
his right hand across her back,

her left hand lightly on his shoulders.
to spin, she kicks out — an elegant *patada,*
as if her foot could orbit the sun. out of practice,
they laugh as the music turns before they do.

she had abandoned the dance — once,
she had gone alone to this *milonga,* such
beautiful men sought her eyes for a permission
to ask & she had turned away, her fear, a soft hiss

in the drums' brushes. she had fled
the crowded floor. tonight, the music wraps
them in satin, stitches their hands together.
the music ends, & she curls her leg around his —

they hold the position. their lines deny gravity
the *cuartas,* a balanchine perfection.

13. FARRAGO

how the adrenaline slips away
as they leave the *milonga* —
on the walk home, few words,
a mist, the street lights haloing.

an insect chorus as they walk
thru the garden to her red door.
he turns, seizes her shoulders,
almost terrified — a snake knotting

his throat until he speaks & the hiss
drifts away, lost in the garden's night choir
and hum. his proposal halting,
a farrago of words falling from his mouth

like rain, and she answers, *yes, yes,
yes!* her words whisper & tumble.
then she laughs, arching her back,
& in a brief *colgada,* dances

with him over the threshold.
nueva salida — a new beginning.

EPILOGUE

the photo has been folded in his wallet & unfolded
till no pigment remains in the creases. he has clipped
it to the fridge, a magnet quoting *neruda,*
there was grief & ruins & you were the miracle,

flattening the bottom — in the photo,
he is taller, clothed in a tuxedo of shadows,
she, also taller, but always less tall
than he, her dress a lighter gray,

a flared skirt. her face tilted upward,
his gazing down, their profiles
chiaroscuro, much younger, radiant —

their bodies arched for the fall,
& then the catch, for the *volcado.*

NOTES:

bandoneón — an accordion-like musical instrument adopted by tango musicians to create the mournful sounds of the tango

boleo — the whip, a circular motion, abruptly changing direction & the supporting leg turns as the other leg rises with a whipping motion

colgada — hanging, in a state of controlled off-axis

giros — a turning step

lustrada — shine, stroking a man's pant leg with a shoe

media luna — half moon, sweeping motion of the foot usually danced by the woman

milonga — may refer to the dance salon where people go to dance tango or to a tango party

planeo — glide, one dancer steps forward, pivots with the other leg gliding behind as their partner dances around them

promenade — walking by facing the same direction and stepping forward while embraced

sentada — sit, the woman creates the illusion of sitting on the man's leg

volcado — a falling step: the man causes the woman to fall off her axis before he catches her; requires the support of a close embrace

BODY LANGUAGE

SMALL TASTE

if I became rain instead of wren
& fell into your hands —
a small taste of desire.

to be the dream & you the sleeper
in pines, our empire — night murmur,
owl song, cicada's bright hum.

or I the sleeper & you the dream,
the mountain pass, a guardrail undulating,
the promise of flight, the falling —

in this dream, you are the cat,
prose glistening along your back,
a flick of tail, story of touch & stroke.

in a cyclone of possessions & downpour,
the thunder roiling, the wind a pike,
our plates & forks whirling in the yard,

I lose my feet in the morning fog,
the strand with its pipers & scatter of shells,
the wash of wave, horizon of swords.

I become the gibbous moon,
a swell of longing, drift of light.

BODY LANGUAGE 1

I have been talking to my body
lately, questioning her decisions
to blunder along in my veins like
like a runaway horse, tying muscles
into intricate celtic knots,
waking me at 3 a.m.,
responding to changes
in barometric pressure
like a drunken rhino.

if I say, *I couldn't live like that,*
my body, stubborn alien hiding
in my vertebrae, says, *yes you can,*
& writes a serial drama that ends
with me — living like that.

a foreigner, my body,
a secret troll who only listens
enough to plot against me,
would just as soon
prick my finger as throw
a table leg into my shin!

in my mind, I am an 18-year-old,
but wiser than that careless co-ed,
& deserve a body that matches.
my body says it doesn't forget.
if I step off a curb into a vacuum,
my body records the incident,
plays it back on rainy days,
visits the body shop where

a sullen mechanic fashions little daggers
to aim at targets etched on every joint.

I ask my body to find pleasure,
& she says she doesn't remember that,
becomes almost deaf if I inquire
about the reason for her rebellions.
c'mon, I say, *get up & dance.*

BODY LANGUAGE 2

my body showed me pictures
today — my skin, transparent,
my bones, transient white shadows.

with her hysterical muscles,
her tantrums & tortures,
she protests the invasion
of one bone spur, as small
as a hang nail, lurking
in the exam room —
she waits to scrapbook this
noirish image of my hip.

body, you are teaching me
about the universe,
its ligaments & muscled sky,
its elusive limbs —
how each element
knots & twines
on its way to the next
depot of pain, with

my will collapsing
in each spark
& murmurous explosion.

body — teach me
about gravity & falling,
how a tendon outstretched
has bound me to the stars.

BREAKING NEWS: OFFICER SLAIN

when a police officer is killed,
my body remembers
my days of waiting,
ticking off his zone, his shift,
my muscles curling
around adrenaline,
fear like a caul
until the phone rings
& he says he is fine.

even now, without him
sitting in my kitchen,
or sharing my bed,
& working the midnight shift —
even now, I startle
at that breaking news,
dissemble & wait
for a phone, its ring.

flesh does not forget —
rends my breath,
plunders my heartbeat,
& in this fragile
moment, stutters a sigh
from the hollows
near my heart.

in my veins, that vibration,
a ringing phone, a prayer born
of an old grief for the fallen.

A MISSED-THE-POINT KIND OF GIRL,

& in the end, the point was sharpened
& plunged deeply, a wordless persuasion.
all you feared is written on your chart
& you, meaning I, cannot read the diagnosis,
or parse the future tense of what is happening

now! so many afternoons,
you came as an impostor, not you,
in second person, but indefinite you,
really me, sobbing at the end of the movie,
watching lovers reunited like I
should have been, but you demurred
& moved out & on, & the heroine is
a memory of what romance
could be if you would just shut your eyes
& dream — dream & drive,
dream & wash a single dish
five times, as the daydream fucks
with your opening paragraph —

& who will you be after all the doors
are closed, after you have shed the disguise
of the invisible, or its opposite — it may be
too late to be whoever it is that you are, a definitely
indefinite pronoun, a chrysalis or perhaps
a phoenix, but not if ashes are involved
or fire that leaves charred love letters
in a rusting metal drum, burning while
those ashen quote marks drift into the pines,
saying goodbye with a smoky grammar,
a blistering third person kind of desertion,

the only way to achieve a first person
singular encryption of lost love left to die,
that lazy cousin of commitment — you must
embrace yourself, become a feathered thing,
write a last paragraph about wings & hope —
if not, you will find despair's lioness waiting
for you, meaning me, & my indefinite self,
& she will consume you, or me, maybe
they, meaning you will stand as witness.

BEACH GIRL

on the beach
in my mind
always tan,
pink bikini
me

music loud, beat
& blur, dance
floor dark & foul,
drunk & wild

electric blood
shock of heart
beat & cheat & blur,
two timing
me

sunset drink
goodbye soon,
a snapshot
of the gulf,
not me

listen, murmur
mermaid songs
sonata for
a recluse,
maybe
me

YES, #METOO

but, not the details —
as I keep stalling
in the middle
of that paragraph.

what I didn't
know at 13 —
my young confusions —
my eyes fallen shut.

it was virginal,
vaginal.
a tear that caught
& splayed across
my left cheek.

the kitchen floor,
hard & gritty,
a dusty noodle
under the stove.

AFTER THIS,

I will be who
I was — wild,
walking swiftly.
after this —

but now,
I am slow
with decisions
to move, made in a brief
unraveling of thought —
perhaps.   perhaps,
I may rise, hobbled phoenix.

2
how rising & healing
changes what remains
after this,

memories of blankets
so heavy, immovable
objects falling,
& their awkward retrieval.

the wish to forget this time,
but to always remember
that what now is out of reach
will always be a gift.

3
after this, I may unwrap
one hundred years —
my mind its
own universe
of past poured
over dreams

I will be in my little house.
a wren, its black down & feathers
once scattered in my bedroom,
will haunt the closets,
& my old dolls reclining on the shelf
will be heroines in buckskin
or maybe crinolines a mile wide.

one hundred years of sleep,
of waking to a day of bathing
my magnificent sagging skin,
of patting dry its damp glisten,
pulling on attire for adventure -
how far is it to xanadu or boston?

4
after this,
the dome of morning still
will rise among the eastern pines
amber & lilac light
burning away the darkness.

& I will wake & rise
so easily, but remember
this morning, the resistance
of muscle, its tug & pull,
the triumph of gravity,
my sweet ally.

5
after this,
when I recall my friend
& her forgiveness, I shall say
a prayer for the path to be walked
if she opens the gate, not just
for mercy's key that
first turned in the lock.

6
when the water oak slowly turns
golden, shedding the waxy green leaves
unfurled last spring, her naked arms
embrace the winter sky
& pelt the roof with acorns —
after this, tiny missives, seeds
of promise, spark of life.

7

after this, a flame dances
undefined. a brittle burning guess,
which limb will dance or pratfall,
& lose my precious luck —

can I call the unknown brutal?
or rebel against its silence, beg
for clairvoyance, see clearly a time
when pain is an afterthought?

oh luck, give me
cat feet in dark halls,
the blessings of friendship,
the tender touch of offspring.

8

after this, again, & again
fingers of morning begin
too early, the shades drawn
in perpetual twilight could dissuade me
of sunrise lofting into the pines,
shutting down
the great owl's hunt
before its prey cries out.

to wake in darkness,
night murmurs still
hung in the dew-strewn
hedges like morning matins,

rising voices for the new day
coming, yet delayed by time's
fey cruelty, its dark thread
raveled till dawn.

9
before this, in that time
of entangled hours,
I knew a man who
wanted to kiss me,
undo me.
he lavished words
about the kiss
when we met in the garden
of a quiet museum,
orchids ghosting & dangling
around us, their spiny petals
reaching out — it would be
like this he said, his hand
waving toward the blossoms,
dancing ladies, spiders
& moths, daggers
& golden showers —
the air misting,
delicate on my skin.

I did not trust him
& walked away.
but the words!
oh the words!

10
another day offers itself —
anthem for a blank page
of prose or asemic praise

for dawn on the other side
of the house, its light
invisible to me until I move —
that squeaky operetta,
potential breakdown,

my body encumbered,
dozing till midmorning,
lets dawn slip away —
the sun strikes the shades,
midday, scribbling
hieroglyphics across
the rug, a summons
for the living.

11
after this, chrysalis unfolds,
wings patterned like snow drifts
cat's paw soft & white
on my cheek, before sunrise,
an elegant waking.

BODY LANGUAGE 4

body, I am still giving
way to suggestion,
to the overlap of fantasy
& over the counter
magic — a bargain if I take
it home, fumbling keys,
parsing the long narrative
of succumbing.

as you sing
an aria to walking,
I radiate electric zings,
twinge when twisting, regret
the shock of full rotation.

when will you give in?
a bride without her dress, silk
lost in a musty wedding chapel,
an extravagance that radiates
with cracking bones
instead of that soft rustle.

body, I am waking
to an avalanche of aching,
a fear of falling.
will you keep me
or betray me — this mind
that loves you?

YIN YANG

1.
when I feel transparent
& dream of dressing
in a bedsheet kind of couture,
like a mannequin with no eyes,
arms severed or twisted
into the pretzeled physique
of an imaginary, seductive
yet harmless body,
a helpless secret.

2.
the fallen leaves scud
down the driveway
snapping beneath my feet
on my way to the mailbox,
a jazz fest of percussion,
& the black cat, dozing
under a tangle
of azaleas, is content —
the familiar like an embrace.

THE KITE ELEGIES

1.
if my bones were hollow
& my heart a kite
I might trifle with clouds,
shake my tail of torn sheets
& twine, charm the wind
to lift me pas de deux
into the sky, a dance
with hawks & dragons,
tissue paper pulse & crackle.
you might be my tether,
my hillside,
or I may cleave to
the wind & snap
the delicate cord
that binds us

2.
my heart, the kite
soars a mile into
the clouds (cirrus
strangers sighing
at the end of the bar,
smoke rings thundering,
flickering neon — auroras
singing a last embrace)
I am a dancing paper bird
an origami swan, fierce
& unfettered, drifting
into trouble.

3.
trouble begins with a hole
in your heart, a rip, if you are paper,

& when rain cascades across
your body, you will fall,
bridle twisting, rag tail heavy,
a brutish storm.

I kiss the sun, but still
descend in an awkward tango,
spine yielding to the devil
in the wind, spiraling
like leaves in autumn
before they scatter
on pavement.

on impact, sparks fly
from the power line & I
who danced in the clouds,
a wonder of lift & grace,
crash in an oak tree,
my tail raveled
& bridle, cut,
no more face,
just bamboo
struts & spine
not kite, not heart,
just evidence of gravity.

4.
old kite string
wrapped around
an oak branch
for so long, it has
embedded in the bark,

the struts & spine
lost — tinder or trash —

but this string,
after that first rain,
lightning, thunder
shredding the sky,
its loosened tangle
landing bebop rag-
doll — after the fall,
first twig, then bough.

A CORNER OF THE ROOM

you are the corner of this room
with its cracked ebony surface.
you are percussion. today

you are piano & I am silence.
yesterday you were the silence
& I was color, paint & luminance,

lavender & deep prussian blue.
our sky flat in my hands,
no words, just chiaroscuro,

my deepest shadow rising silently
from the chair, & now I move
ungracefully in the dance studio.

you are a waltz & I am counting
on my fingers, performing a
stuttering ballet as I step into sunshine

shaped by a clerestory window
& revealing dust motes
that dance with no effort.

now I am splayed on pillows.
you are two hands creating jazz.
I dream the sound as you

touch the keys, as neurons
roam my body, like the music
of the piper at the gates of dawn —

later, no memory of the song,
just the sweet hollow left
where it was sung.

AT TWILIGHT

visit me in the winter of summer —
the windows frosted, the outside hum
muffled by glass & AC rumble.
visit me as the drift of robin song
stretches across the vague light
of afternoon. climb into my bed

when the traffic has slowed
on the interstate & a distant train
horns into the damp air as it passes.
come to my door & step over the cat.
she sleeps there, awaiting your arrival.
come when twilight lies before us.

enter through the kitchen door
while rain pounds the driveway
& washes a slush of fallen azalea
blossoms into the shadowed carport.
from the darkened hall, summon me —
your mute hands now speaking

to me of skin & touch — the lamps
dimmed, footfall quiet even when
we shift to the kitchen. stay for supper.
uncork the wine & slice the shallots.
linger with your glass tipped toward
the candlelight. stay the night.

FOR JIM,

Jim Morrison, pardoned on Dec. 9, 2010 for the alleged "Miami Incident" at The Doors concert in Dinner Key Auditorium on Mar. 1, 1969

who was an hour late,
whose tan leather pants were tight, so tight,
who couldn't remember the words,
who has been forgiven
for a trespass we may have missed
because we left early, losing patience
with his drunken stumbling across the stage,
who was still cursing
when we discovered our car
was not where we parked it
at the coconut grove yacht club,
had been towed to the impound lot
in south dade,
who was still on stage,
ambiguous tan leather
snaking around the microphone
as we hitchhiked down u.s. 1
to south miami.

I wish I remembered more

about that long expensive night,
could tell you who picked us up —
four aggravated college students
walking backward for the first time.
or how the railroad tracks
were shining under the miami moon
almost full, how blonde I was, that week,

or whether my short skirt was black
or red or tight, so tight.

or about another night,
when I listened to side one
of *the doors* for hours
as the album played over & over
& the sex was slick & so compelling
we couldn't stop to flip the record,
& the needle kept dropping on "light my fire."
I can hear jim's voice, the organ's pitch
in that darkened upstairs apartment,
can feel the wash of rock & sex,
but not remember the face of the boy
who owned the record.
how we couldn't stop,
& the night stretched out
on cushions parting like waves
beneath me, & the keyboard's pound
propelled us, hands in the fire,
blaze of bodies bewitched by sound,
& we couldn't stop.

& years later, how I listened
to the album on the road,
& couldn't stop
or change the tape,
& wondered why
he was late & drunk,
& who was with me
when the lyrics slurred

across the stage
of the *dinner key auditorium.*
& how I never hitchhiked again,
& six months after the concert
married someone
who didn't know me,
& didn't know how to stop,
even if it wasn't me beneath him —
who was also drunk & late
too often.

how I hadn't played *the doors* again
until he left me shuttered in another town,
& I began again to tempt the fire,
& heard the same song,
a radical pulse beating against
the auditorium's metal roof.

the same fierce anthem —
whoever kissed me.

THIS IS NOT A DIALOGUE WITH TIME,

only a memory of compressing
minutes exponentially,
losing anxious days,
their disappearance —
a howling, holy whisper
of atoms giving way to lust —
a tick-tock lover, a thief.

how a soul becomes transient,
so easily disintegrating —
exhaled breath over a cup
of coffee, smudge of lipstick
on the rim, heaven steaming

in your kiss — that holy ether
now fixed in my marrow,
your taste in little flits of recall.
never again wholly myself,
your legacy of bone and sweat,

all you touched, sloughed off
by now, though new skin recalls
our encounters — memories
dancing wildly in contra lines —
too many changes,
too many lefts & rights.

a delicate narration remains on each
bed & chair, impossible to hold
on to my self, always listening for
that tick-tock lover, that thief.

WHAT IF WE WERE ONE,

in a valley of touch, the terrain
a marriage shaped by hard wind.

if we were one, my face,
its aging pallor, would
still be cherished — our lives,
like pages in sacred books
turned carefully with white gloves,
pressed roses between the chapters.

& if the knotted wonder
of our souls became breath
& breath became ash —
our ash in an urn,
its flash of fire,
our story illuminated.

how serenely this dream has fallen
into the center of my heart —
the core of our hands,
fingers interlocked,
fists of anger fallen loose
as we honor the sacrament
preserved in each wondrous cell.

ON THE OCCASION OF YOUR BIRTH,

I did not know that your luminous skin would toughen,
your face so like mine would change, would beard,
the razor nicking as you taught yourself to shave,
the mutter of surprise, the sting of styptic pencil.

I did not know when you danced with raggedy ann
that you would later lose yourself in heavy metal
& the secret musings of mazzy star —
earbuds buzzing in the kitchen,
head rocking as you loaded the dishwasher,
dreaming of jack kerouac & robert pirsig,
that you would compose a poem
that made me weep, its delicate beauty —
that you would face the world
without defense, with armor broken,

that driving through mountain passes, you would love
the rocks that rise above the somber clouds like fathers,
that you would marry in a church in late september,
shop for groceries, cook dinner after work,
assemble a snow blower in your dank garage.

I did not know that you would grow to be a man,
choose to live in the mountains,
& drive on ice across this savage world.

INK

I am finally writing this letter,
I apologize for my forgetfulness —
so thoughtless to leave my pen
silent, our conversation unfinished.

this pen now seems loquacious —
      words, words & little
      birds in the margins
hopping onto the page.
how does this pen know me?
trailing all the threads of my life
on paper, the paper
inhaling each stroke
grasping at the ink with hunger,

recalling birth & wanting you
to remember that hour,
swaddled & nursing.
can a fragment still burn
from the midnight of your first day?

there was a twilight
in the hospital,
every one dozing,
except you, squirming
free of your blanket,
reaching,
still reaching,
even now.

THUNDERSTRUCK

I dreamed I held nothing,
that nothing was here, then
gone — a silver tongued flight artist,
always shrugging, so nonchalant,
whispering those famous sweet nothings,
lingering only to write farewell before fading.

then I held everything,
& everything was heavy
& contradictory, at once —
trying to dance & thread a needle.
everything seen thru the eye, flotsam
crowding every cluttered space.

I dreamed I held love, so weightless,
a delicate thread for the needle,
a dance imposed, a place
for the heart, its muscles torn.
its shadows, glimpsed at the kitchen
window, thunderstruck & beating.

JANUARY 13

memories of water
splashing, a pool,
floating under,
listening to laughter
in that silver fish way,
syllables rise
above the pool,
a cappella joy.

under water,
my suit floating
around me, its tutu skirt
rippling with a ballet swish,
nipples cold,
their silhouettes
jutting thru the nylon,
my flat chest
waiting to bloom
— it would not be
like a flower
but an atomic
cloud rising —

my body, twisting torso,
drop of blood in the water,
osmotic crimson filament
splayed below the surface.

BUS DEPOT

my ex-husband called tonight
still writing his sad list of regrets.

long ago, I sent my anger away —
to a bus depot of despair,
the wait so long, your soul
must leave your body
or it will stiffen & sink
into the bench's
wooden slats, a new ache
with each destination
squawked over the loudspeaker,
telling you it is time to give in,
not take him back,
but abandon that suitcase
of his transgressions
to unclaimed baggage —

call it forgiveness,
or forgetting,
but leave the depot,
paint your bedroom walls
lipstick red & shop for
matching satin sheets.

SKIN

amazed at my skin,
its inevitable collapse,
a transformation
from taut to slack

enlightenment —
its chagrined red glow & blush,
a flash, the last phase
of a magnificent confusion.

my skin, its symbolic whiteness,
its caul of privilege
an inheritance, like pearls.
its scars that recall vertigo

& falling, a murmured
benediction. embraced by
my skin, its endurance in endless
passages of sun & shade.

awed by the translucent skin
of infants, their smooth fingers
just beginning to grasp the light,
& the skin of my parents,

their ashen pallor as they acquiesce
to dying — time's insult & gift.

INSTRUCTIONS FOR MY ATOMS
WHEN THEY SCATTER

become ash, air borne.

find the rim of the sky, its most
brilliant sunset, become its fuchsia,
its celebration, let shadow overtake you.

join a roost of monarchs migrating
across the gulf. ride thermals
on the back of a red tailed hawk.

drift to a steel beam on the eiffel tower,
& switch on all the lights.
illuminate paris — you have the power.

burrow into the hadron collider
& blast my half-life consciousness
into that tunnel at the speed of light,
no lazing after-life for us —

keep moving.

dive into a giant chocolate cake
& immerse your tiny presence
in its dark & swirling sweetness.
navigate the galaxy
the way a dream travels.

choose rebellion,

the unpredictable. avoid
the windows or walls that
confined your vanished body.

WHEN I WAS LOST,

love found me,
a heap of neurons —
& assembled a hand
that lifted me with
every kind word.
a balm, unguent,
healing each distraught
& hopeless thought.

love, keep me
in the circle
of this hand,
this harbor of trees,
this vigilant sky.

WHEN I SAY STAR,

it is infinite, burning,
holy. There are novas
& light, old light
jostled by the past,
before you,
before the
last note quiets
when the air
becomes still.

when I say speck,
it is I who burn. I am
invisible, a watcher

who somehow changes
the star observed,

though it may
have died
before its light
has clothed me —
I am holy.

ABOUT THE AUTHOR

CAROL LYNNE KNIGHT is co-director of Anhinga
Press. She has edited and designed more than 100 literary
publications, including books by Diane Wakoski, Naomi
Shihab Nye, the late Robert Dana and Judith Kitchen.

Her book of poems, *Quantum Entanglement* (Apalachee
Press) was released in 2010. Her poetry has appeared
in *Another Chicago Magazine, Louisiana Literature, Tar River
Review, Poetry Motel, Earth's Daughters, The Ledge, Slipstream,
Broome Review, Comstock Review, Northwest Florida Review,
Epicenter, Redactions, Iconoclast, Epicenter, HazMat, So to Speak,
J, Down in the Dirt, Rivet, Esthetic Apostle, Cagibi, Dime Show
Review, Black Fox Literary Magazine, High Shelf Press, Postcard
Poems and Prose Magazine, Scarlet Leaf Review,* and others. She
is a fellow of the Hambidge Center for the Arts and the
Bowers House.

Born in Traverse City, Michigan, she grew up in South
Florida and graduated from the University of Miami and
Florida State University. She has exhibited drawings,
pottery, sculpture and digital images in the eastern United
States. In other lives, she has worked as an art teacher,
potter, videographer, copy writer, and graphic designer.
She lives in Tallahassee, Florida.